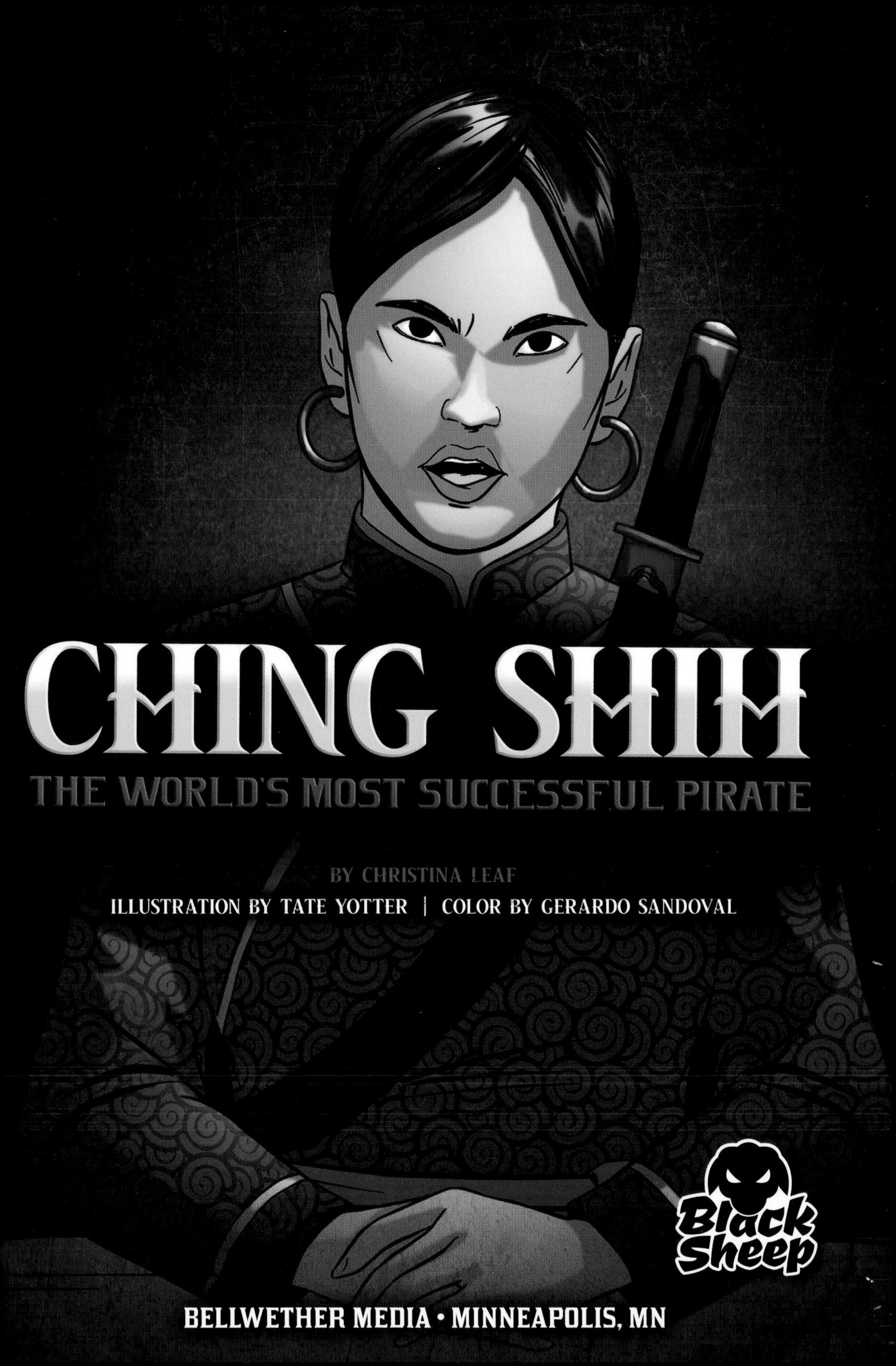

CHING SHIH

THE WORLD'S MOST SUCCESSFUL PIRATE

BY CHRISTINA LEAF

ILLUSTRATION BY TATE YOTTER | COLOR BY GERARDO SANDOVAL

Black Sheep

BELLWETHER MEDIA • MINNEAPOLIS, MN

Stray from regular reads with Black Sheep books. Feel a rush with every read!

This edition first published in 2021 by Bellwether Media, Inc.

Library of Congress Cataloging-in-Publication Data

Names: Leaf, Christina, author.
Title: Ching Shih : the world's most successful pirate / by Christina Leaf.
Other titles: World's most successful pirate
Description: Minneapolis, MN : Bellwether Media, 2021. | Series: Black sheep : pirate tales | Includes bibliographical references and index. | Audience: Ages 7-13 | Audience: Grades 4-6 | Summary: "Exciting illustrations follow events in the life of Ching Shih. The combination of brightly colored panels and leveled text is intended for students in grades 3 through 8"– Provided by publisher.
Identifiers: LCCN 2020017783 (print) | LCCN 2020017784 (ebook) | ISBN 9781644873021 (library binding) | ISBN 9781681038414 (paperback) | ISBN 9781681037592 (ebook)
Subjects: LCSH: Zheng, Shi, 1775-1844. | China–History–Jiaqing, 1796-1820–Biography–Juvenile literature. | Women pirates–China–Biography–Juvenile literature. | Pirates–China–Biography–Juvenile literature. | China–History, Naval–1644-1912–Juvenile literature.
Classification: LCC DS756.23.Z47 L43 2020 (print) | LCC DS756.23.Z47 (ebook) | DDC 910.4/5 [B]–dc23
LC record available at https://lccn.loc.gov/2020017783
LC ebook record available at https://lccn.loc.gov/2020017784

Editor: Betsy Rathburn Designer: Andrea Schneider

Printed in the United States of America, North Mankato, MN.

TABLE OF CONTENTS

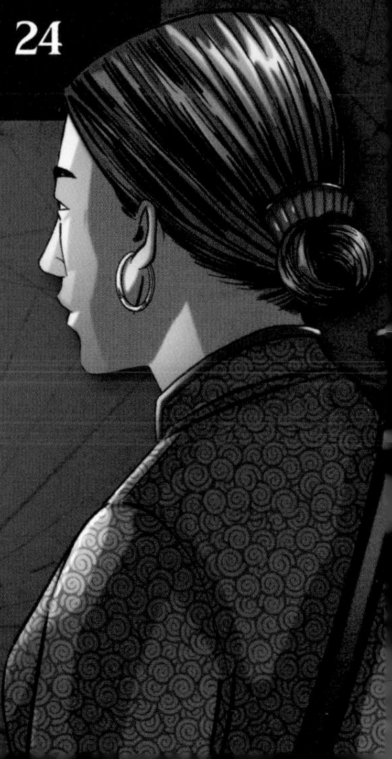

A Woman Leader

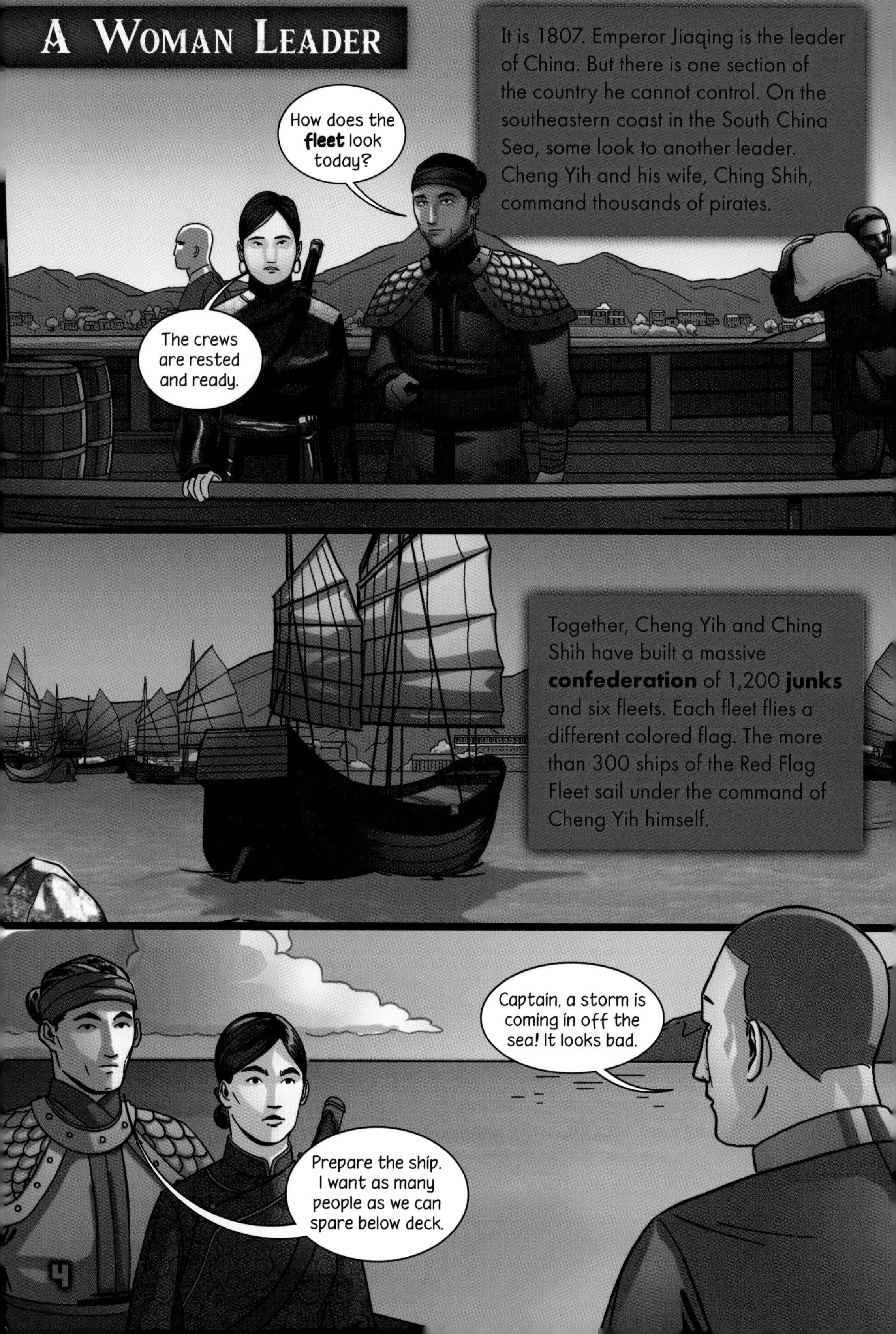
It is 1807. Emperor Jiaqing is the leader of China. But there is one section of the country he cannot control. On the southeastern coast in the South China Sea, some look to another leader. Cheng Yih and his wife, Ching Shih, command thousands of pirates.
How does the **fleet** look today?
The crews are rested and ready.
Together, Cheng Yih and Ching Shih have built a massive **confederation** of 1,200 **junks** and six fleets. Each fleet flies a different colored flag. The more than 300 ships of the Red Flag Fleet sail under the command of Cheng Yih himself.
Captain, a storm is coming in off the sea! It looks bad.
Prepare the ship. I want as many people as we can spare below deck.

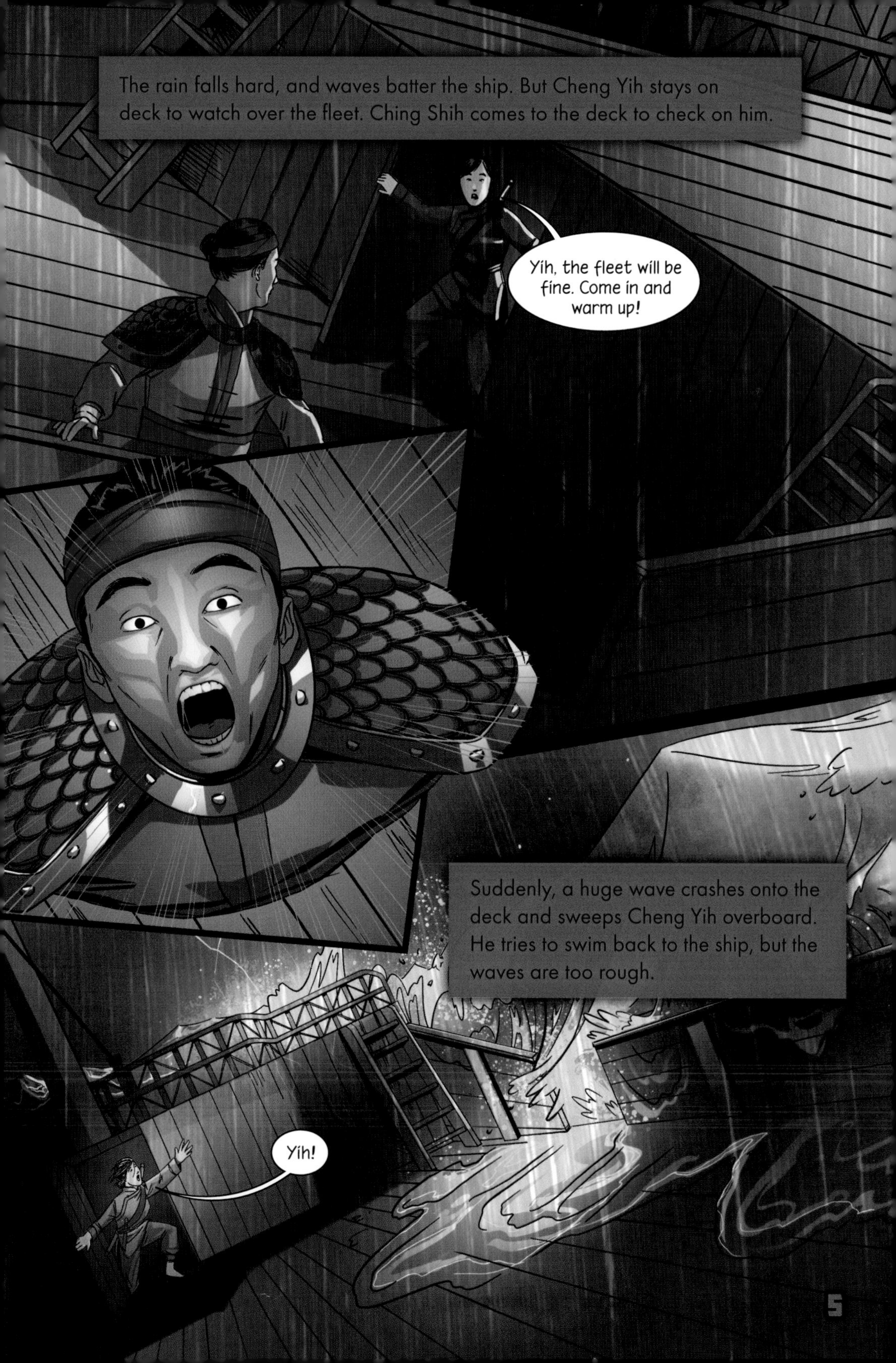
The rain falls hard, and waves batter the ship. But Cheng Yih stays on deck to watch over the fleet. Ching Shih comes to the deck to check on him.
Yih, the fleet will be fine. Come in and warm up!
Suddenly, a huge wave crashes onto the deck and sweeps Cheng Yih overboard. He tries to swim back to the ship, but the waves are too rough.
Yih!

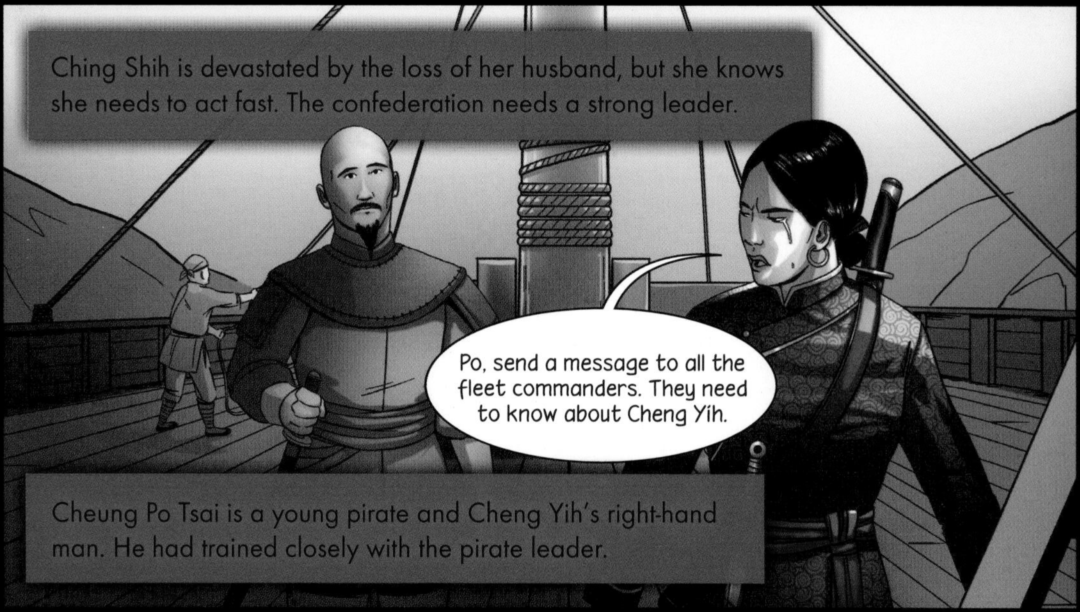
Ching Shih is devastated by the loss of her husband, but she knows she needs to act fast. The confederation needs a strong leader.
Po, send a message to all the fleet commanders. They need to know about Cheng Yih.
Cheung Po Tsai is a young pirate and Cheng Yih's right-hand man. He had trained closely with the pirate leader.

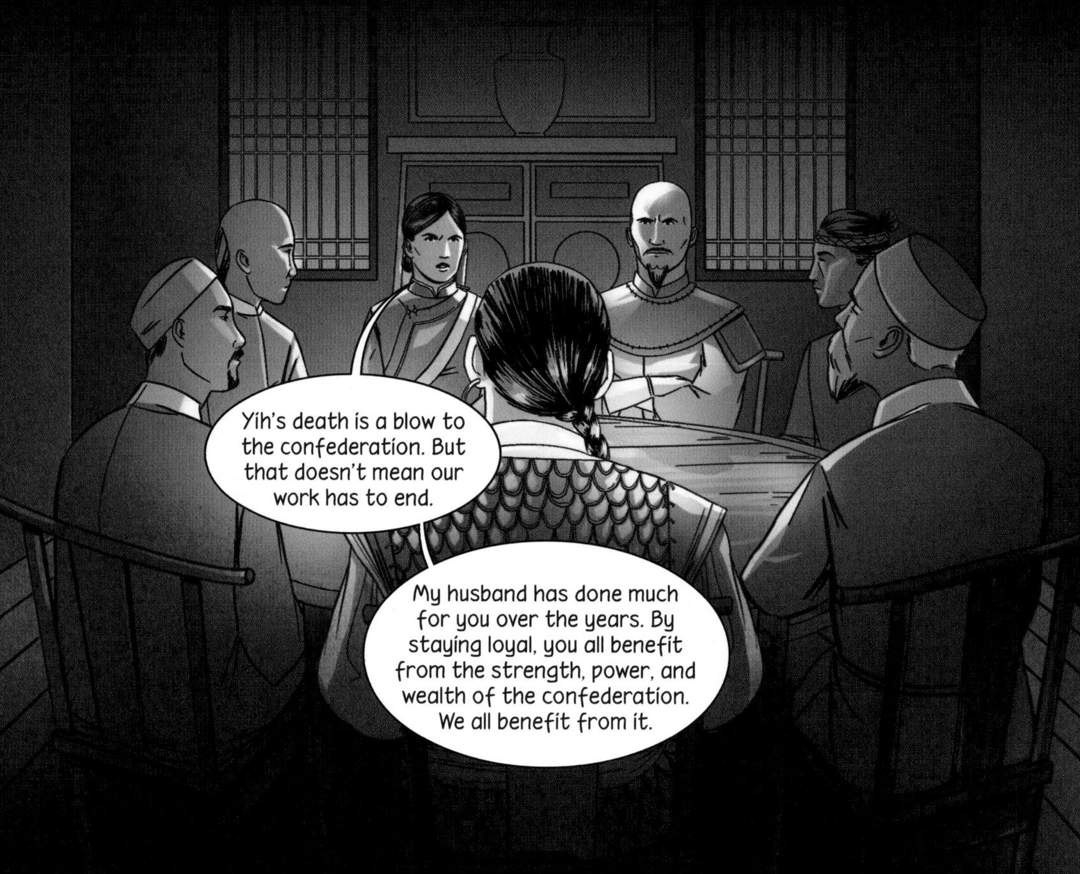
Yih's death is a blow to the confederation. But that doesn't mean our work has to end.
My husband has done much for you over the years. By staying loyal, you all benefit from the strength, power, and wealth of the confederation. We all benefit from it.

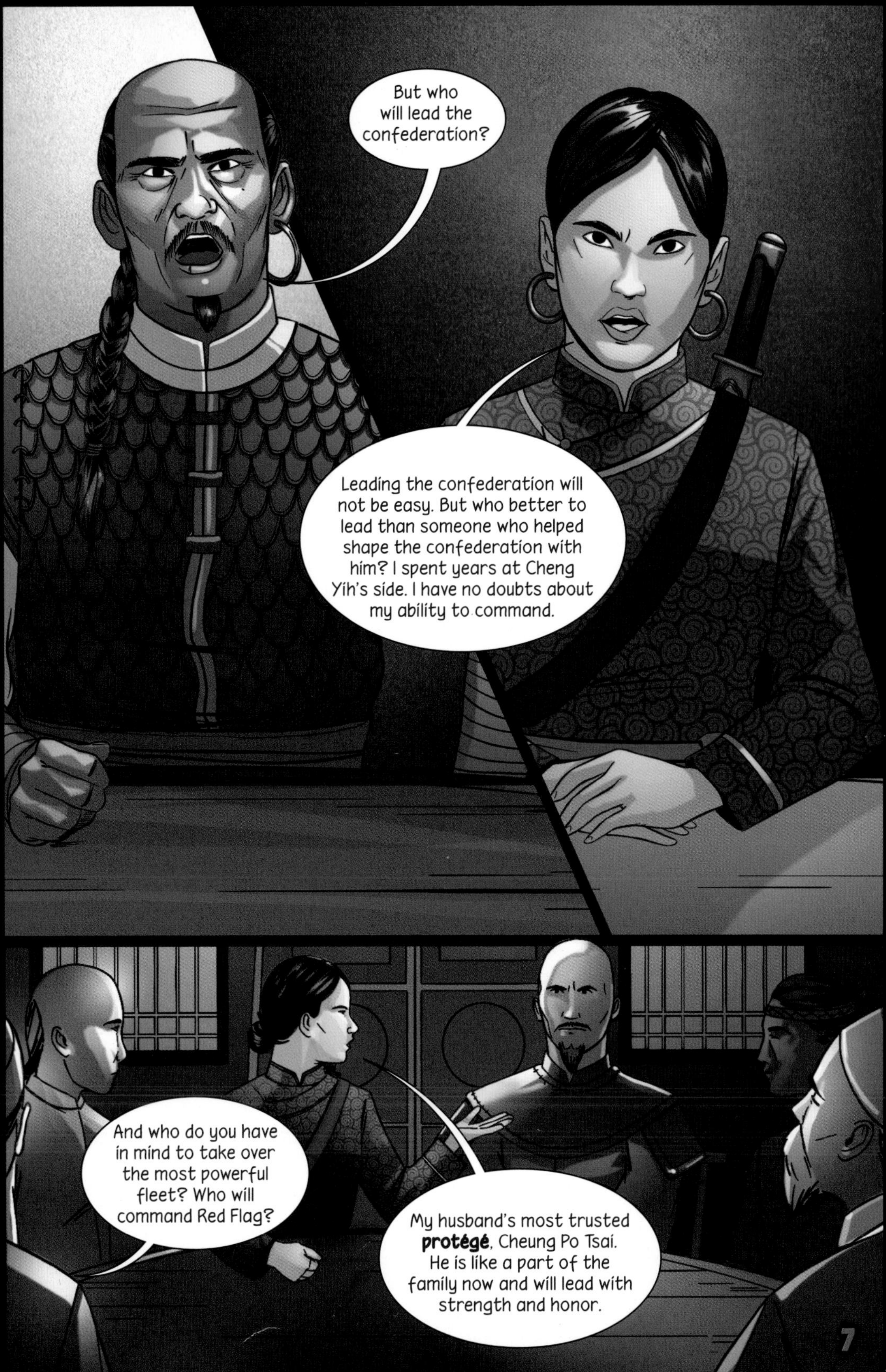
But who will lead the confederation?
Leading the confederation will not be easy. But who better to lead than someone who helped shape the confederation with him? I spent years at Cheng Yih's side. I have no doubts about my ability to command.
And who do you have in mind to take over the most powerful fleet? Who will command Red Flag?
My husband's most trusted **protégé**, Cheung Po Tsai. He is like a part of the family now and will lead with strength and honor.

Taking Charge

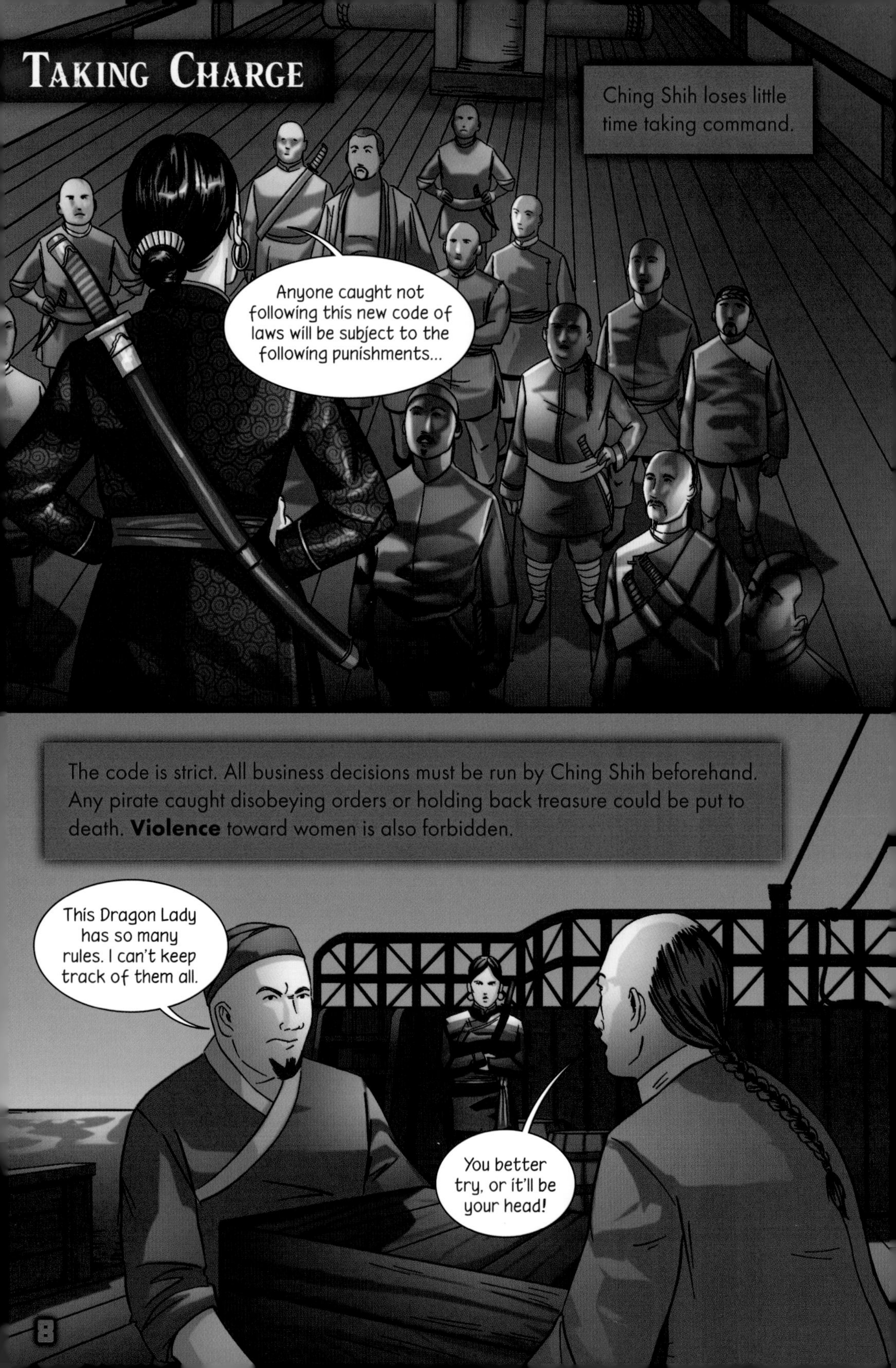
Ching Shih loses little time taking command.
Anyone caught not following this new code of laws will be subject to the following punishments...
The code is strict. All business decisions must be run by Ching Shih beforehand. Any pirate caught disobeying orders or holding back treasure could be put to death. **Violence** toward women is also forbidden.
This Dragon Lady has so many rules. I can't keep track of them all.
You better try, or it'll be your head!

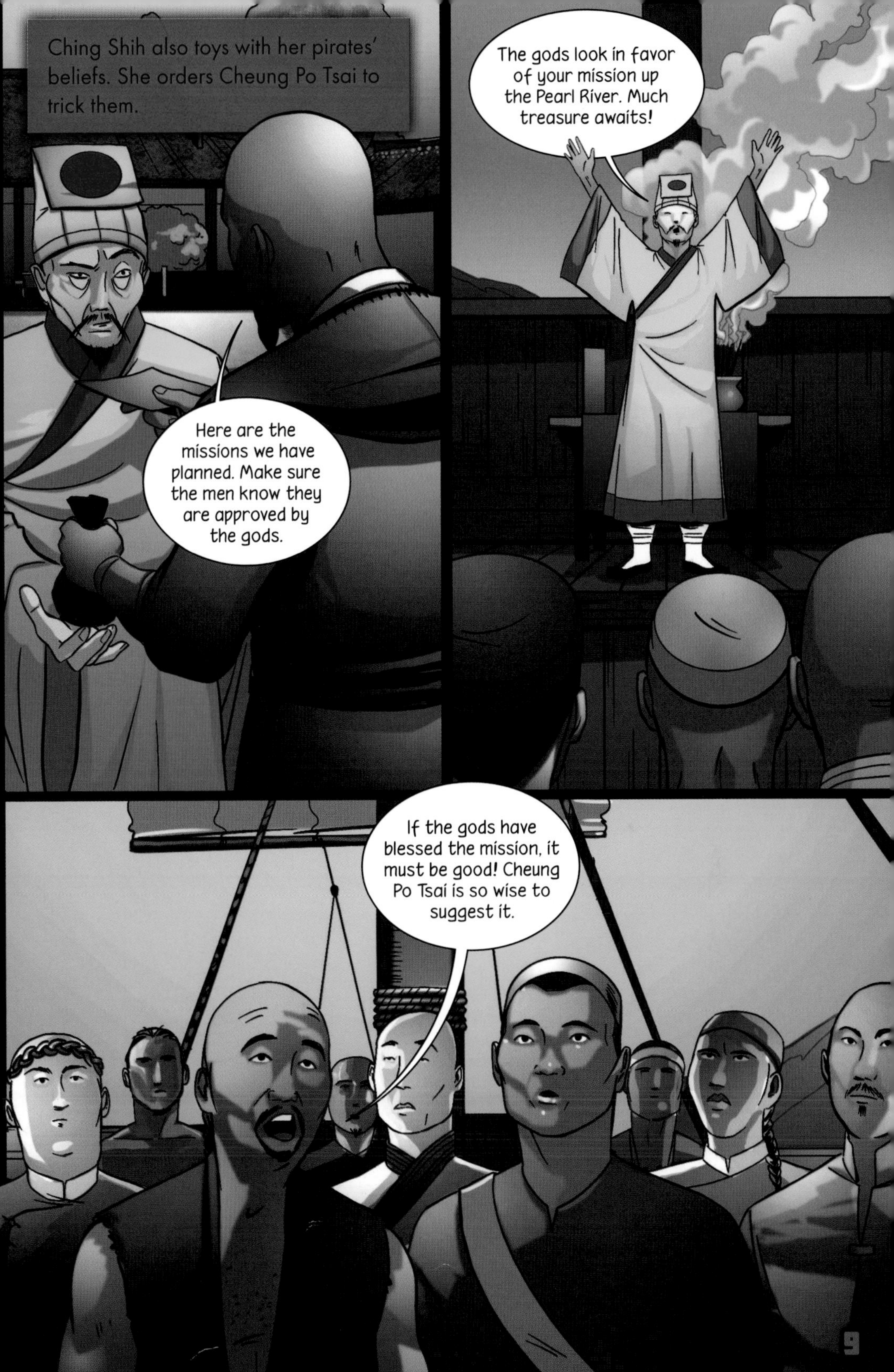
Ching Shih also toys with her pirates' beliefs. She orders Cheung Po Tsai to trick them.
Here are the missions we have planned. Make sure the men know they are approved by the gods.
The gods look in favor of your mission up the Pearl River. Much treasure awaits!
If the gods have blessed the mission, it must be good! Cheung Po Tsai is so wise to suggest it.

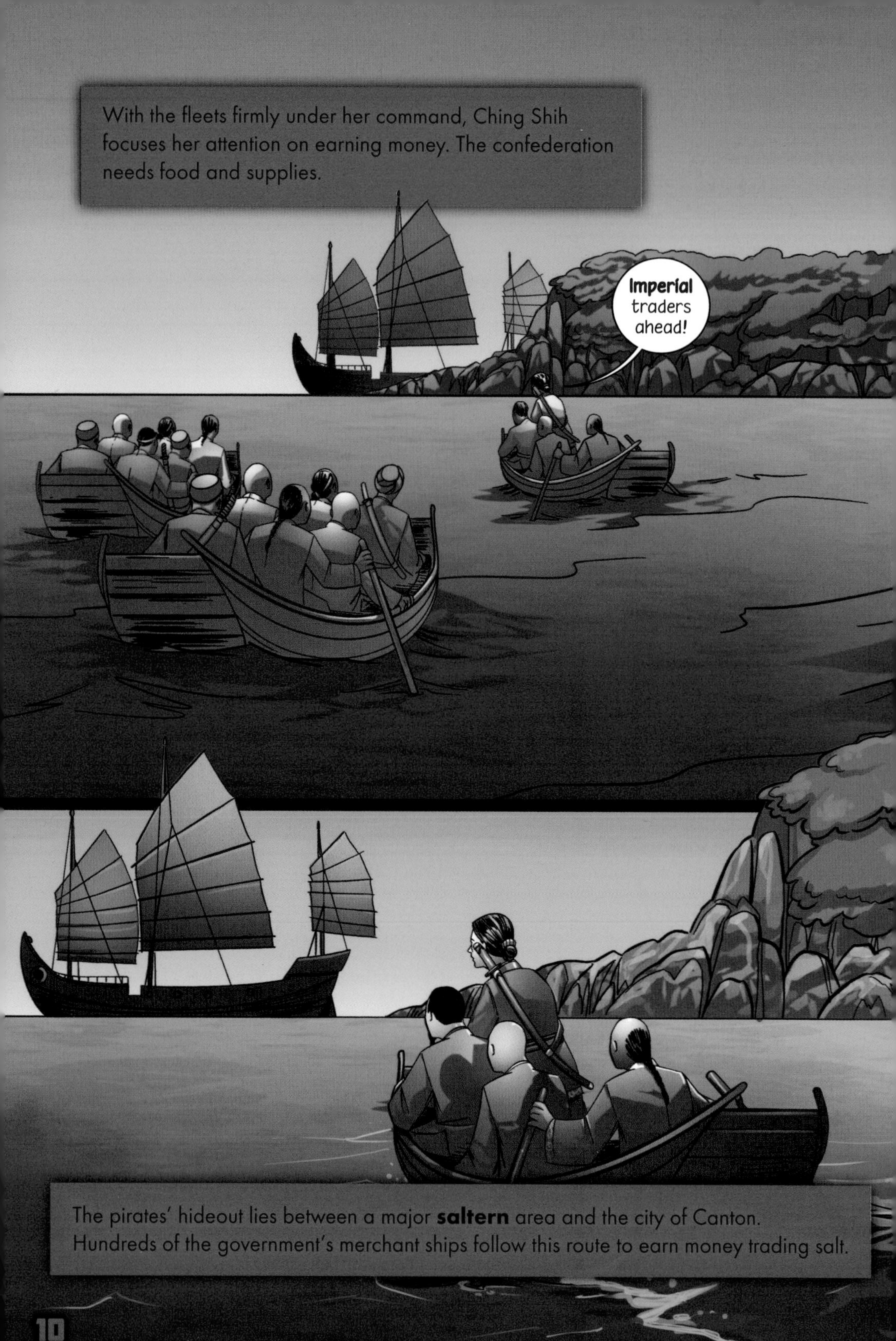
With the fleets firmly under her command, Ching Shih focuses her attention on earning money. The confederation needs food and supplies.
Imperial traders ahead!
The pirates' hideout lies between a major **saltern** area and the city of Canton. Hundreds of the government's merchant ships follow this route to earn money trading salt.

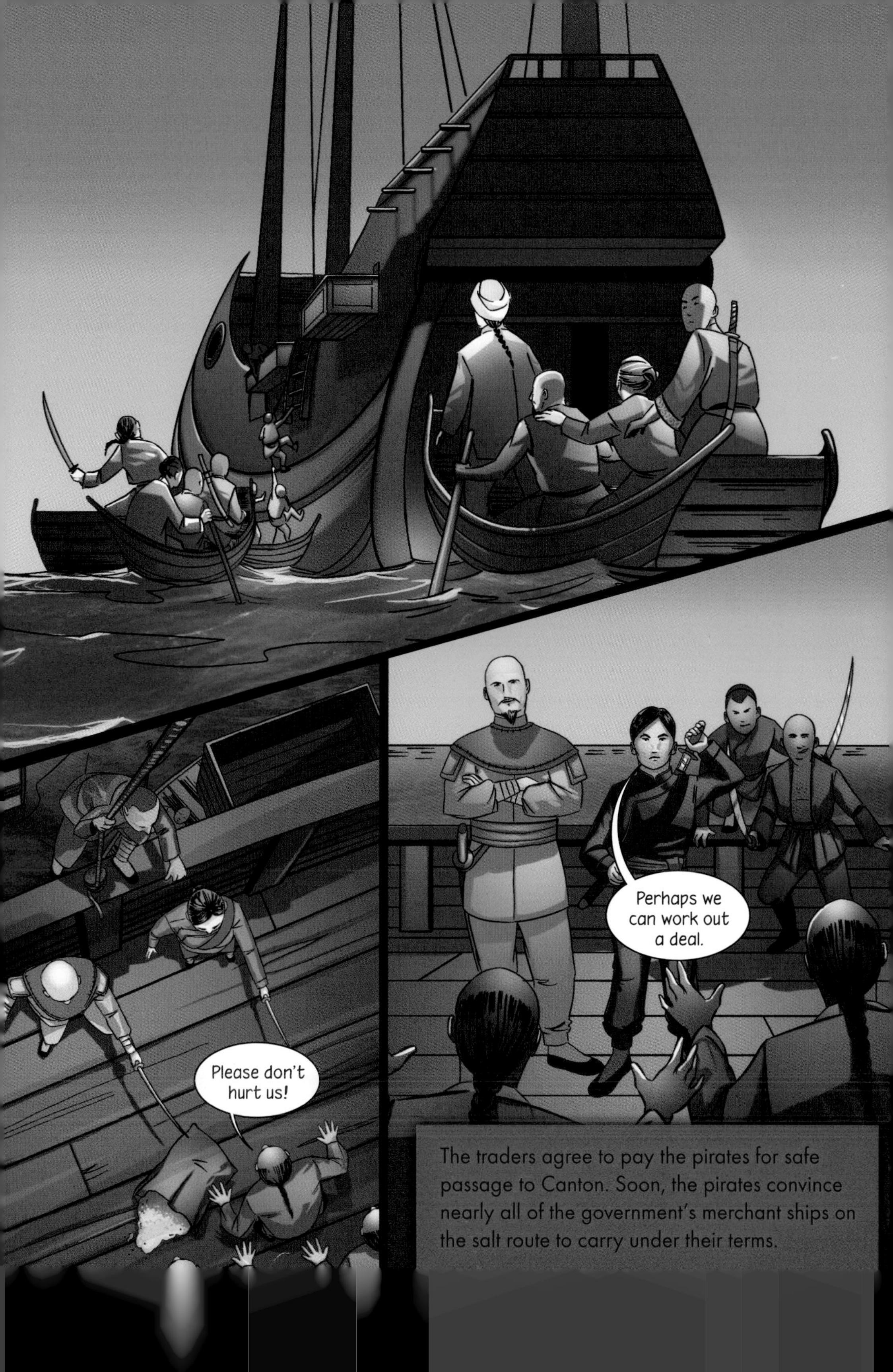
Please don't hurt us!
Perhaps we can work out a deal.
The traders agree to pay the pirates for safe passage to Canton. Soon, the pirates convince nearly all of the government's merchant ships on the salt route to carry under their terms.

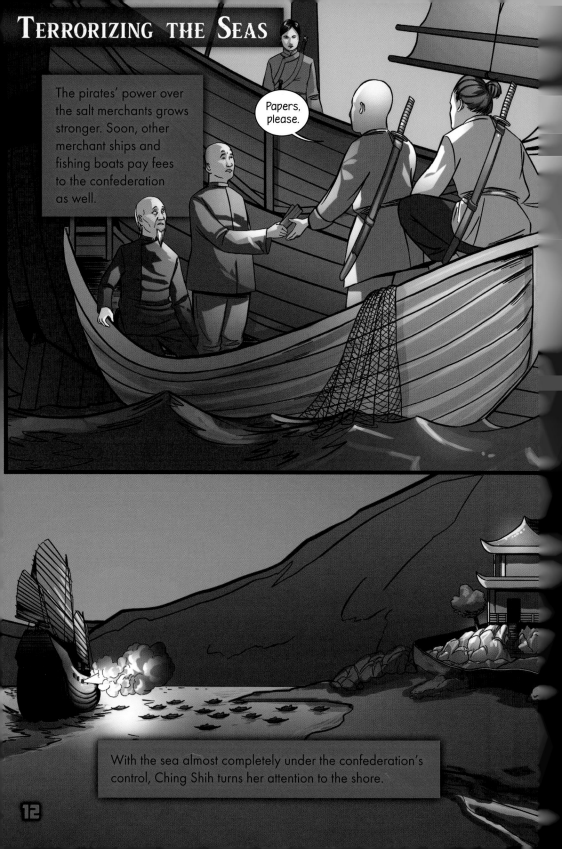

TERRORIZING THE SEAS

The pirates' power over the salt merchants grows stronger. Soon, other merchant ships and fishing boats pay fees to the confederation as well.

Papers, please.

With the sea almost completely under the confederation's control, Ching Shih turns her attention to the shore.

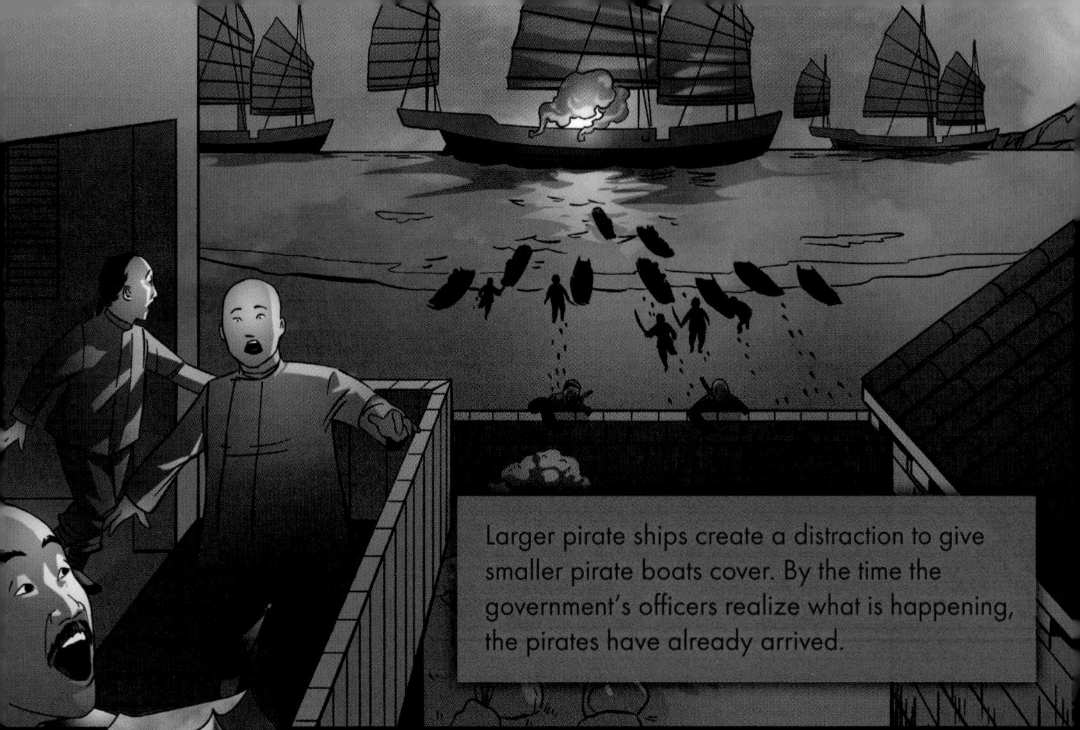
Larger pirate ships create a distraction to give smaller pirate boats cover. By the time the government's officers realize what is happening, the pirates have already arrived.

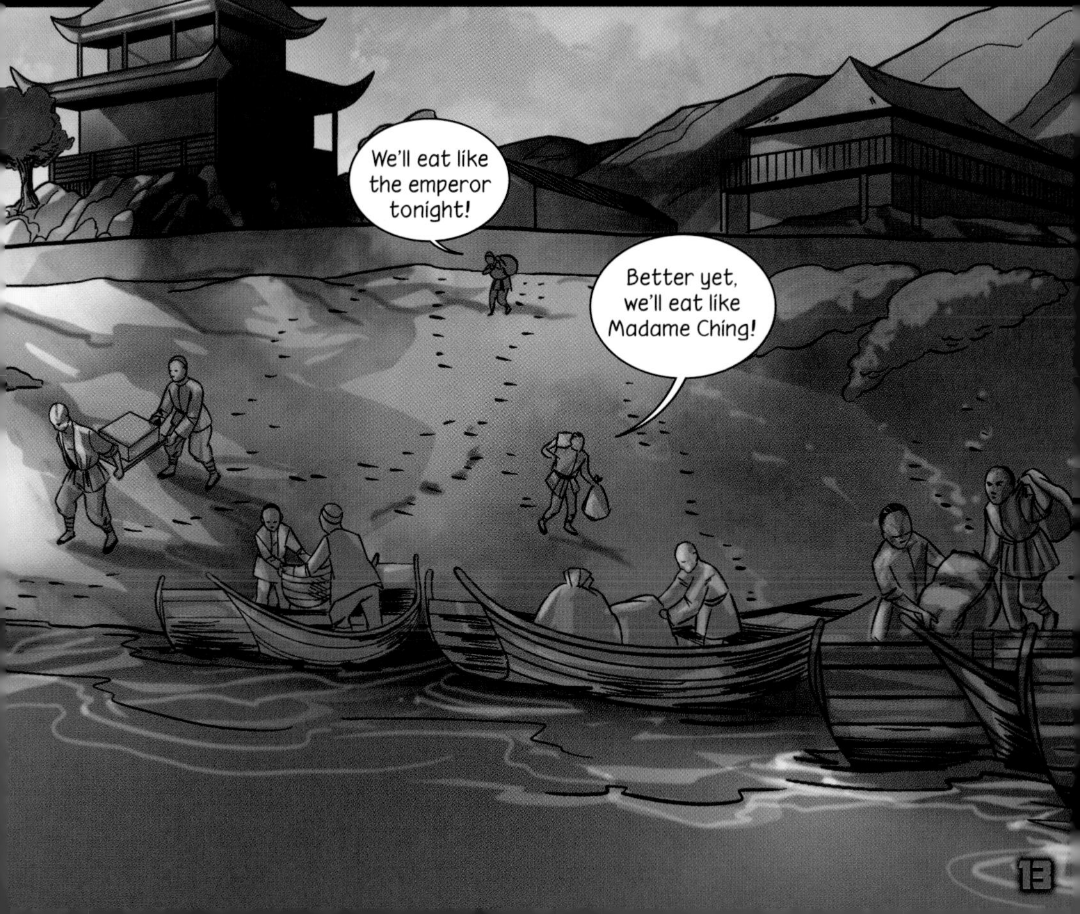
We'll eat like the emperor tonight!
Better yet, we'll eat like Madame Ching!

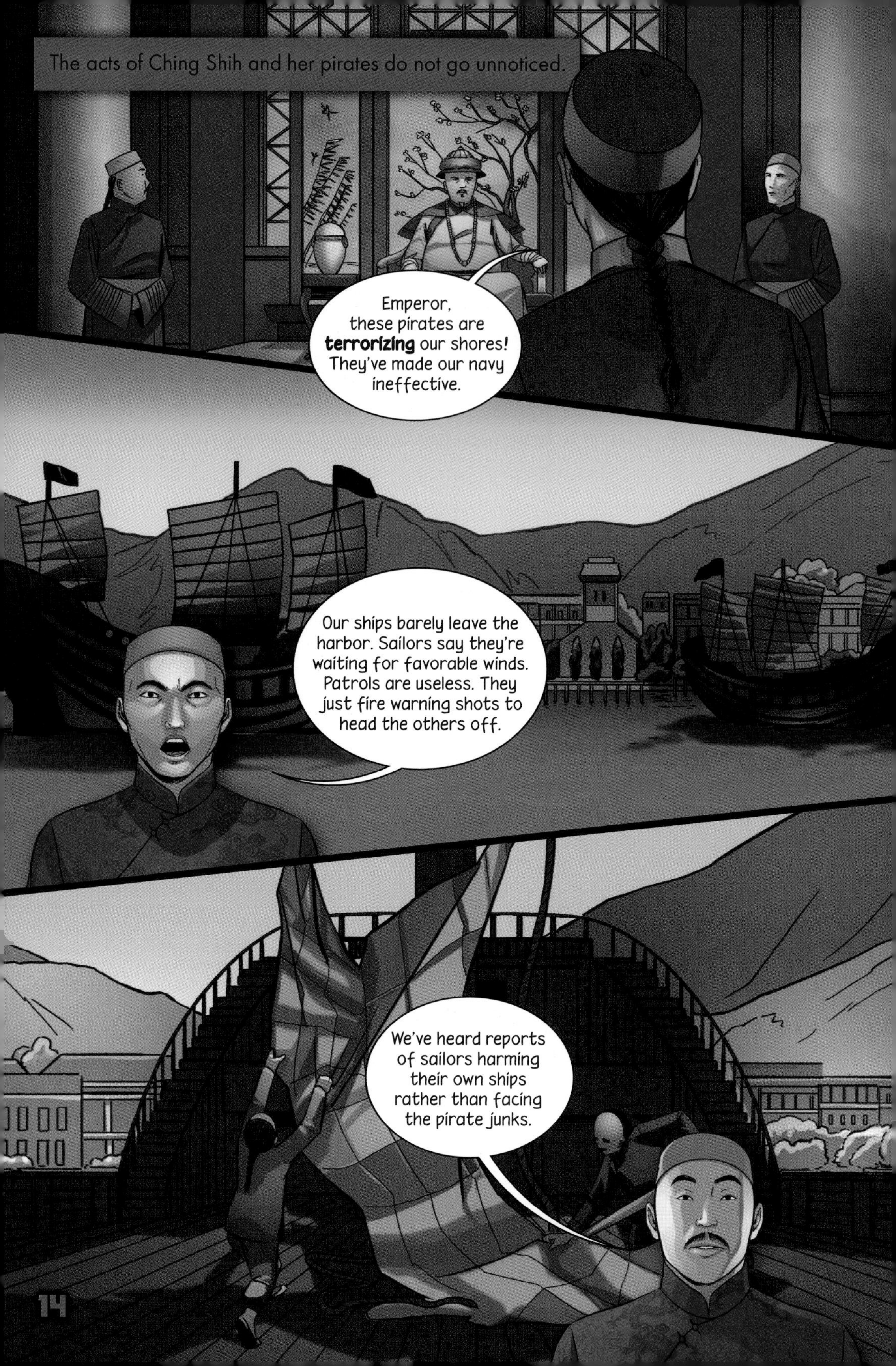

The acts of Ching Shih and her pirates do not go unnoticed.
Emperor, these pirates are **terrorizing** our shores! They've made our navy ineffective.
Our ships barely leave the harbor. Sailors say they're waiting for favorable winds. Patrols are useless. They just fire warning shots to head the others off.
We've heard reports of sailors harming their own ships rather than facing the pirate junks.

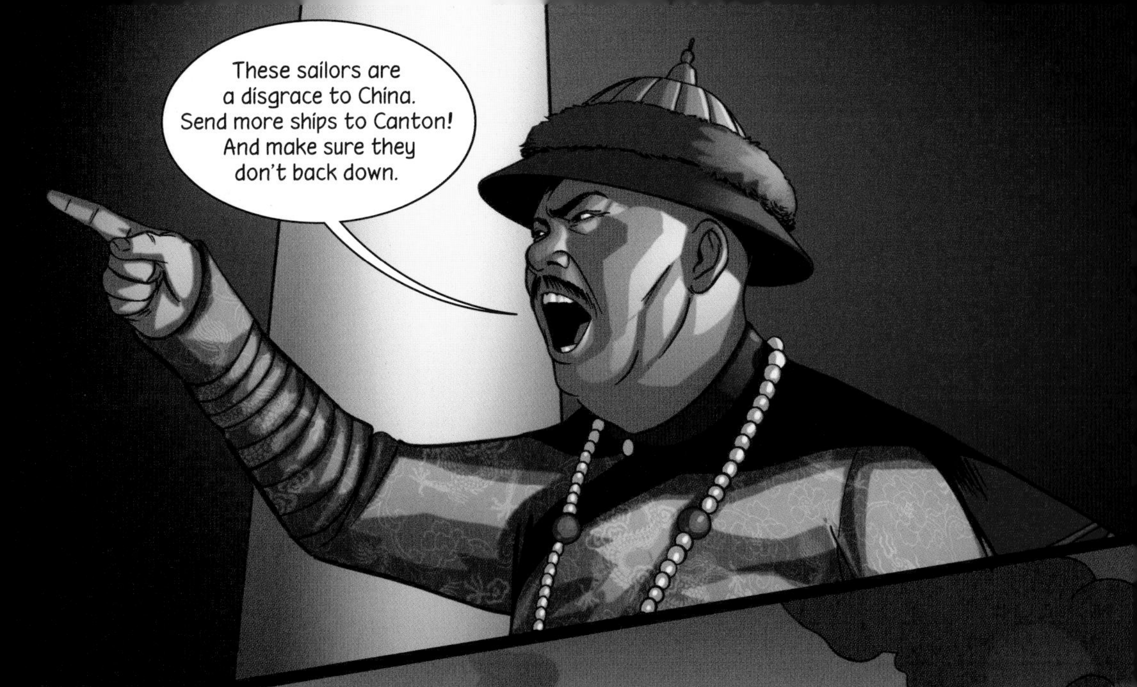
These sailors are a disgrace to China. Send more ships to Canton! And make sure they don't back down.

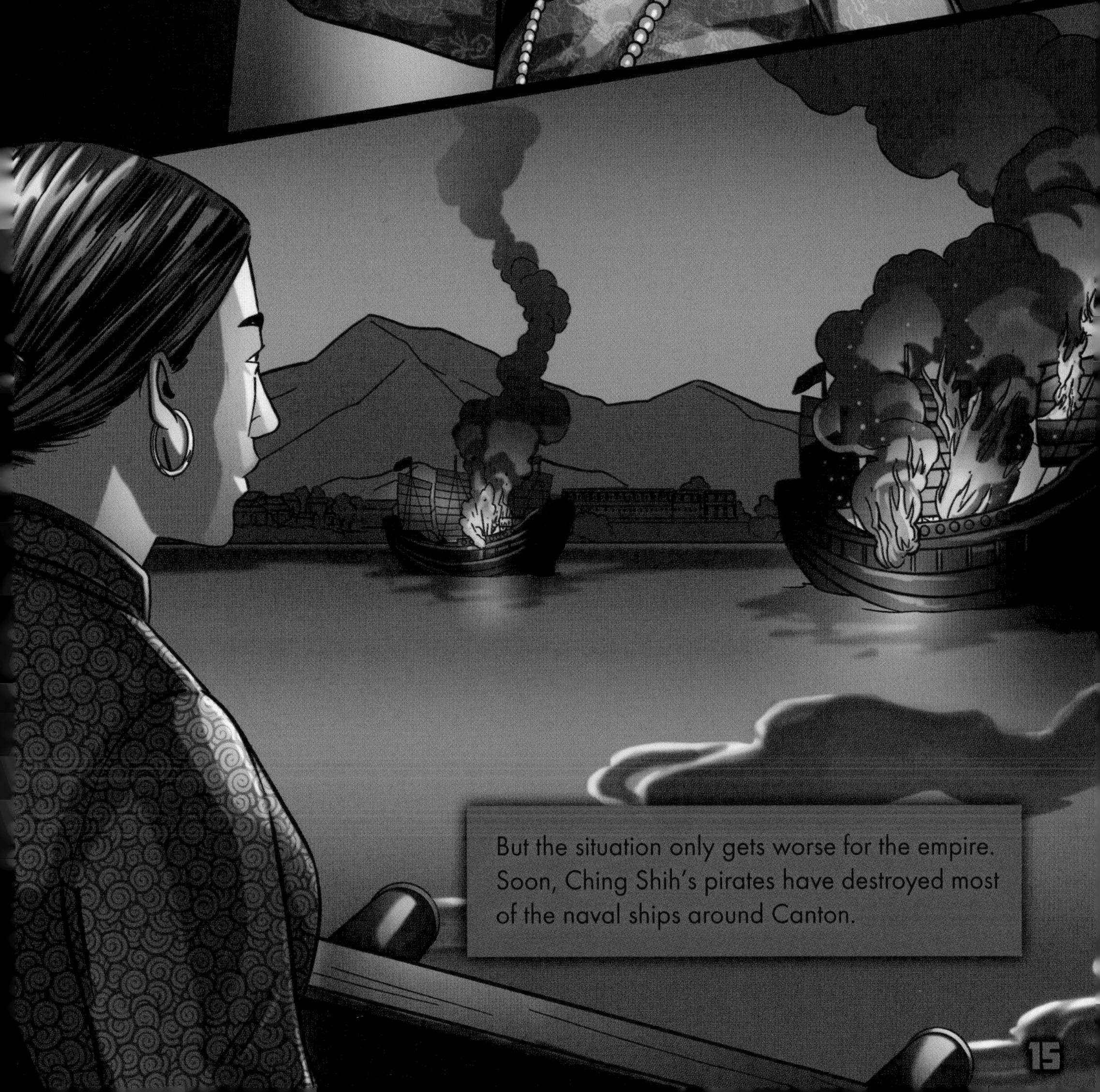
But the situation only gets worse for the empire. Soon, Ching Shih's pirates have destroyed most of the naval ships around Canton.

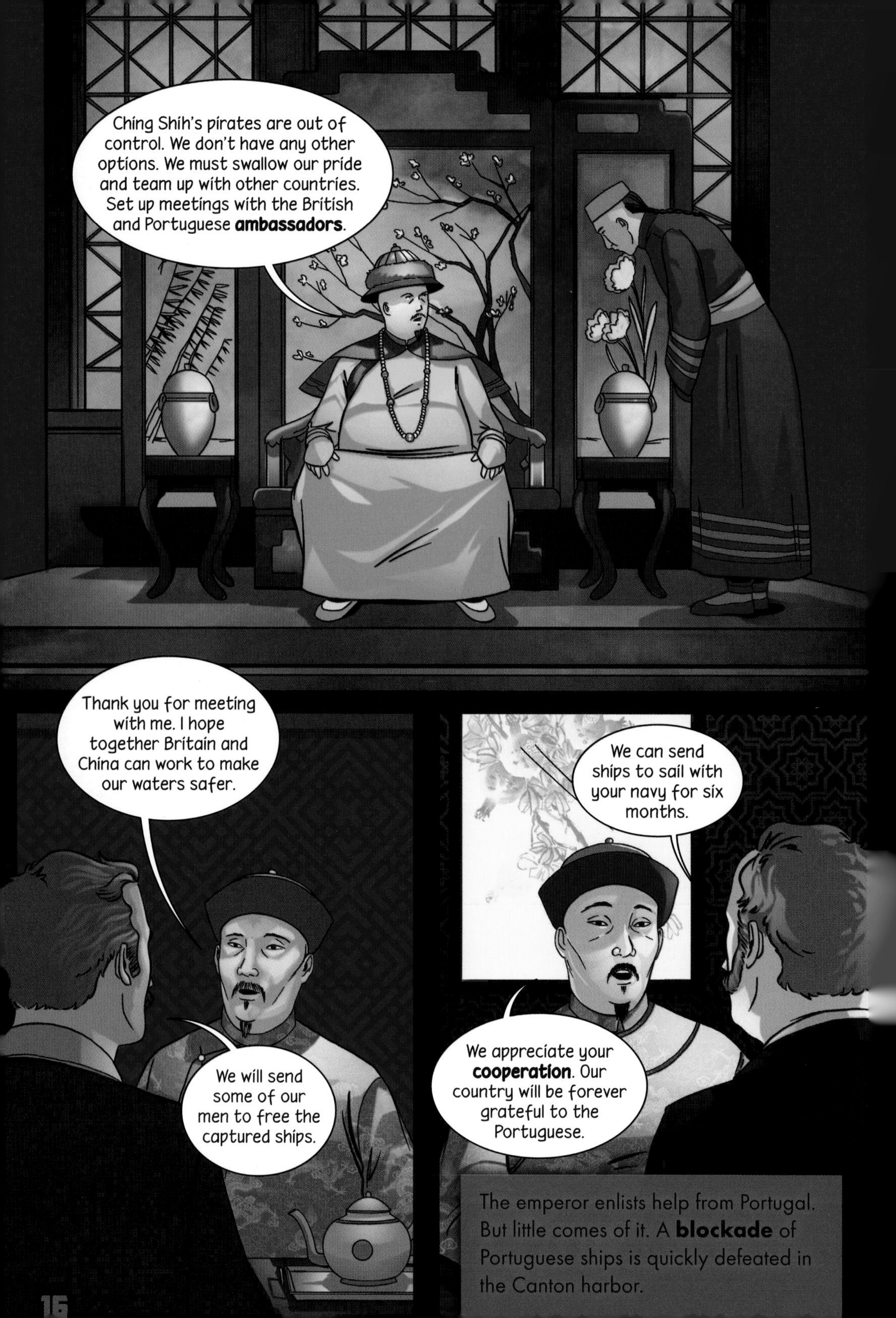
Ching Shih's pirates are out of control. We don't have any other options. We must swallow our pride and team up with other countries. Set up meetings with the British and Portuguese **ambassadors**.
Thank you for meeting with me. I hope together Britain and China can work to make our waters safer.
We will send some of our men to free the captured ships.
We can send ships to sail with your navy for six months.
We appreciate your **cooperation**. Our country will be forever grateful to the Portuguese.
The emperor enlists help from Portugal. But little comes of it. A **blockade** of Portuguese ships is quickly defeated in the Canton harbor.

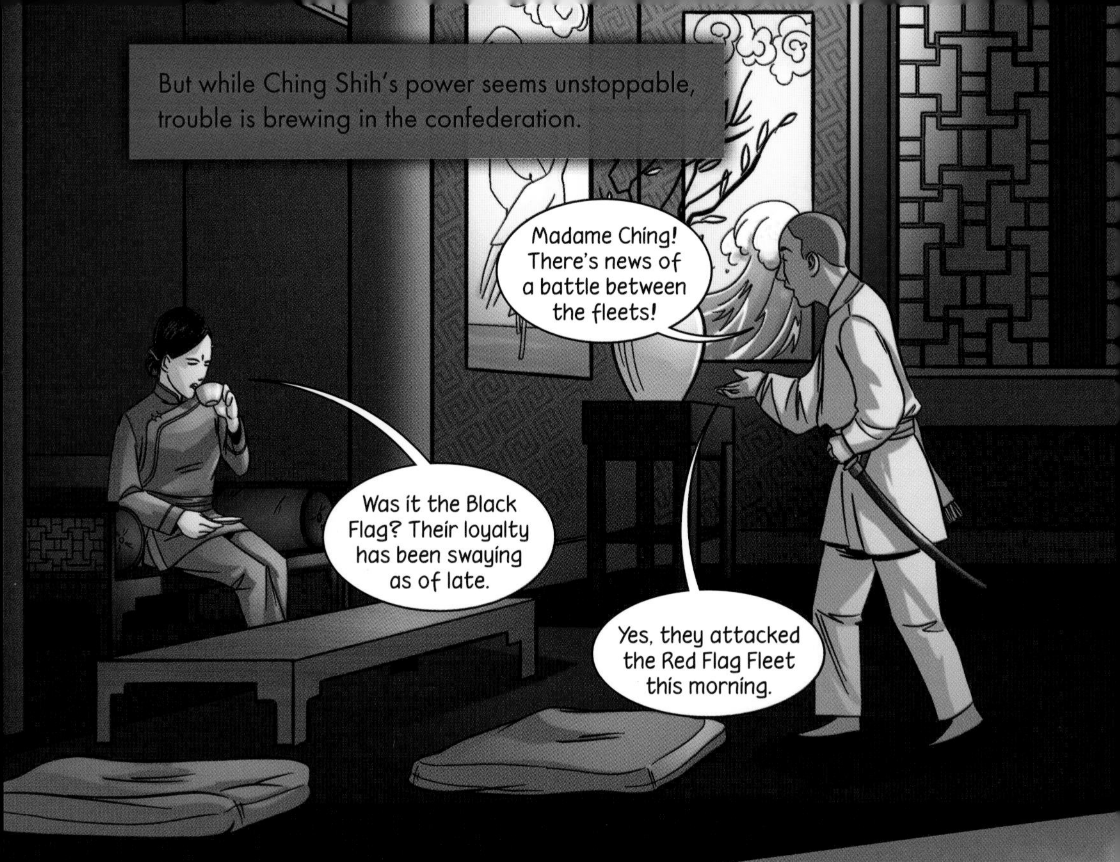

But while Ching Shih's power seems unstoppable, trouble is brewing in the confederation.
Madame Ching! There's news of a battle between the fleets!
Was it the Black Flag? Their loyalty has been swaying as of late.
Yes, they attacked the Red Flag Fleet this morning.

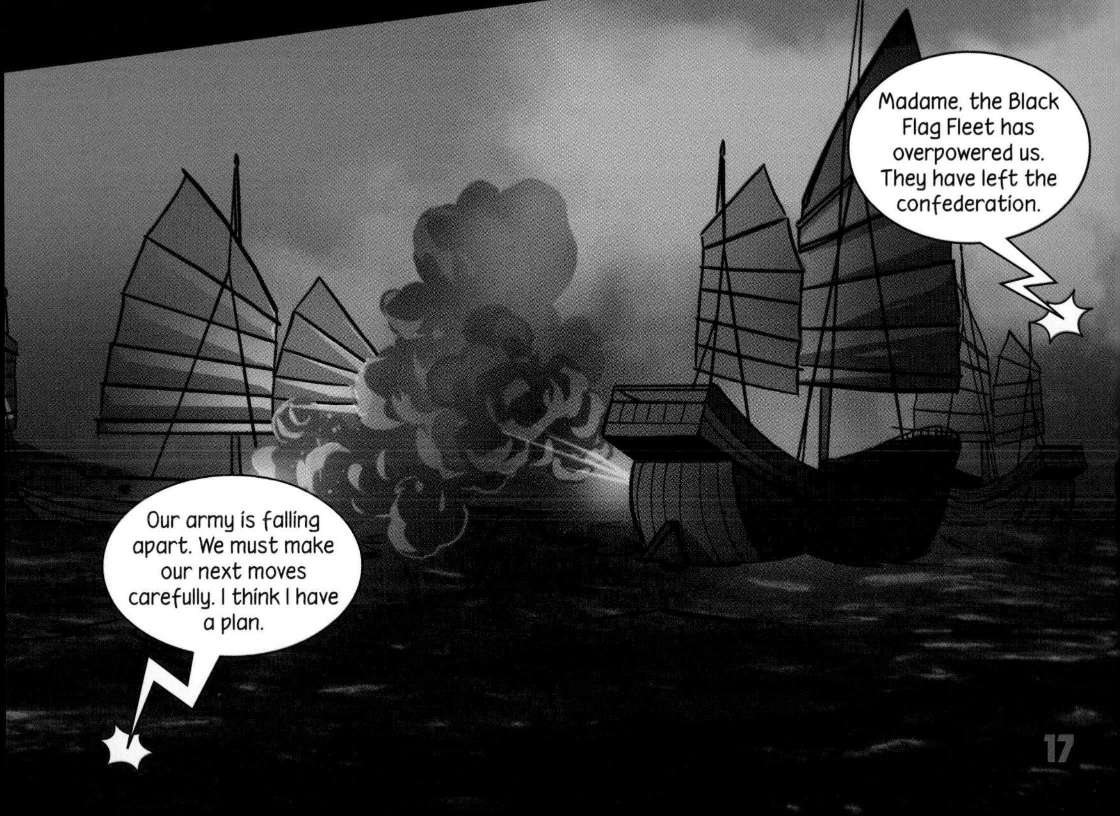

Madame, the Black Flag Fleet has overpowered us. They have left the confederation.
Our army is falling apart. We must make our next moves carefully. I think I have a plan.

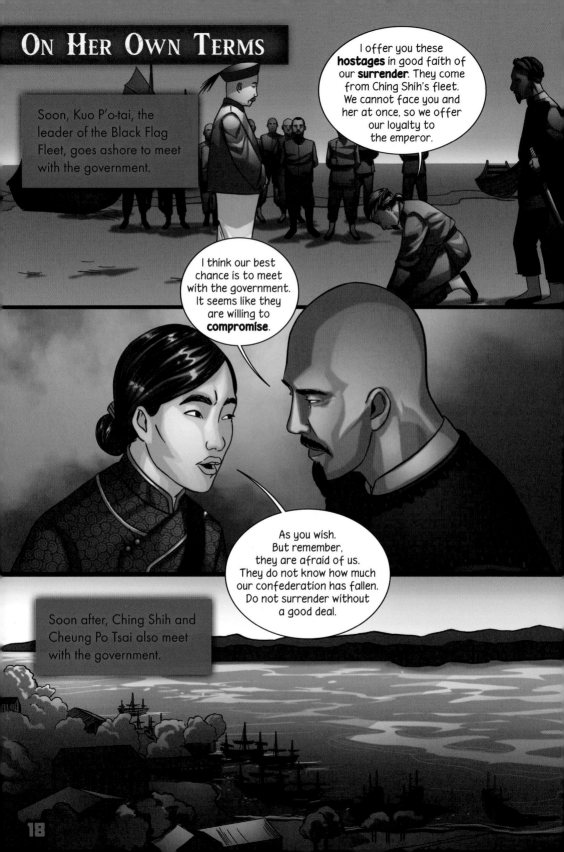

ON HER OWN TERMS

Soon, Kuo P'o-tai, the leader of the Black Flag Fleet, goes ashore to meet with the government.

I offer you these **hostages** in good faith of our **surrender**. They come from Ching Shih's fleet. We cannot face you and her at once, so we offer our loyalty to the emperor.

I think our best chance is to meet with the government. It seems like they are willing to **compromise**.

As you wish. But remember, they are afraid of us. They do not know how much our confederation has fallen. Do not surrender without a good deal.

Soon after, Ching Shih and Cheung Po Tsai also meet with the government.

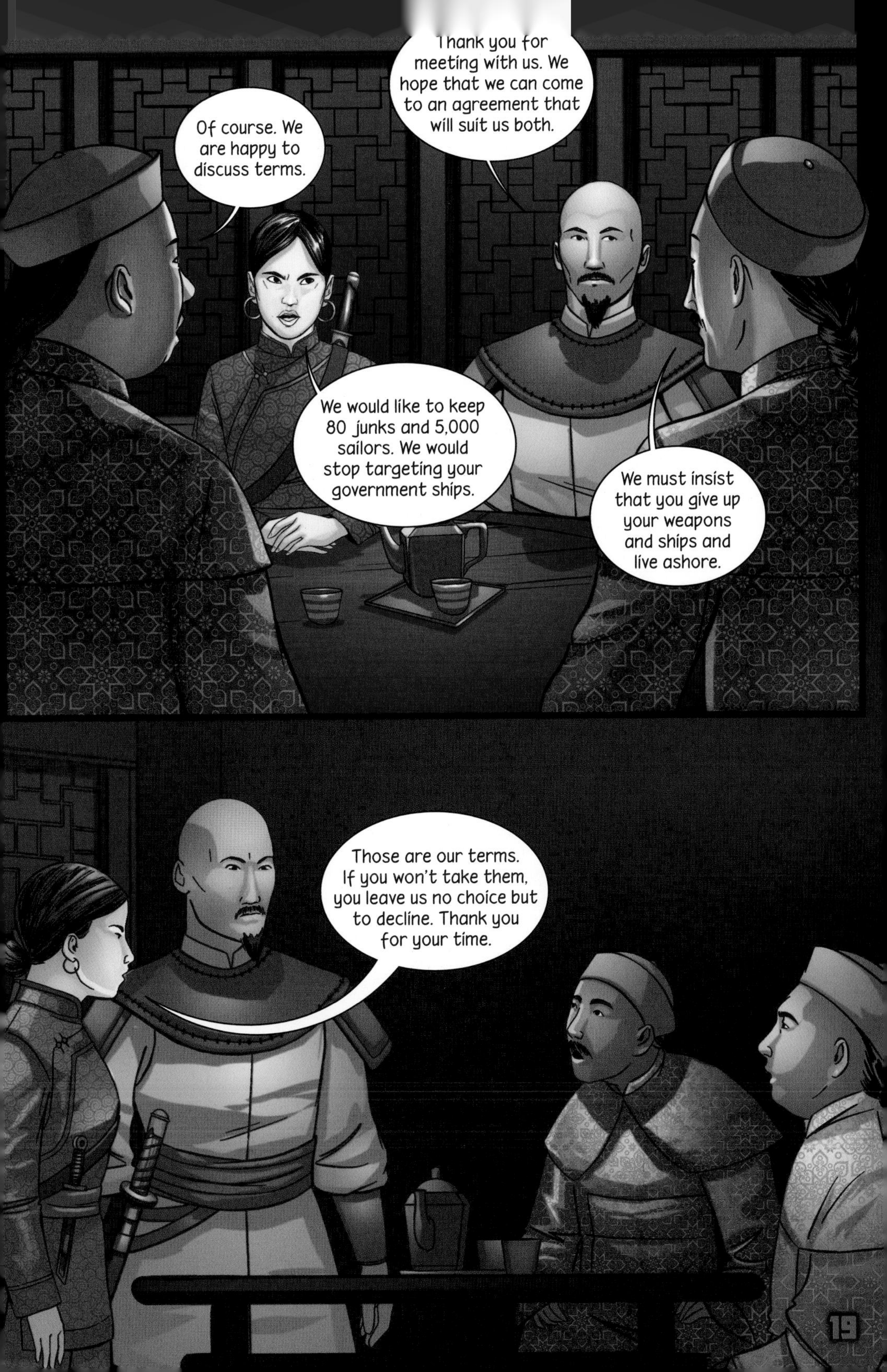
Thank you for meeting with us. We hope that we can come to an agreement that will suit us both.
Of course. We are happy to discuss terms.
We would like to keep 80 junks and 5,000 sailors. We would stop targeting your government ships.
We must insist that you give up your weapons and ships and live ashore.
Those are our terms. If you won't take them, you leave us no choice but to decline. Thank you for your time.

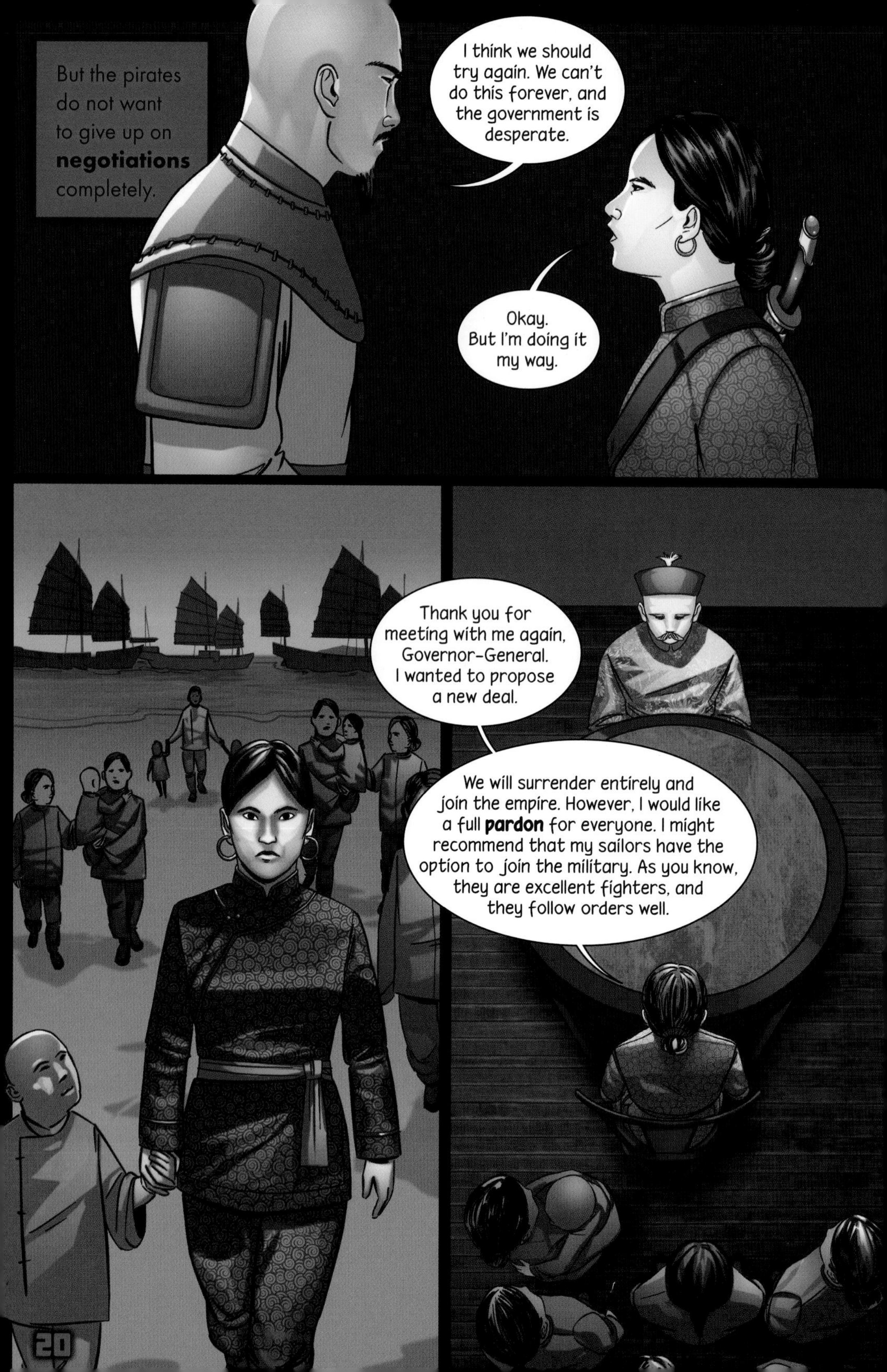

But the pirates do not want to give up on **negotiations** completely.
I think we should try again. We can't do this forever, and the government is desperate.
Okay. But I'm doing it my way.
Thank you for meeting with me again, Governor-General. I wanted to propose a new deal.
We will surrender entirely and join the empire. However, I would like a full **pardon** for everyone. I might recommend that my sailors have the option to join the military. As you know, they are excellent fighters, and they follow orders well.

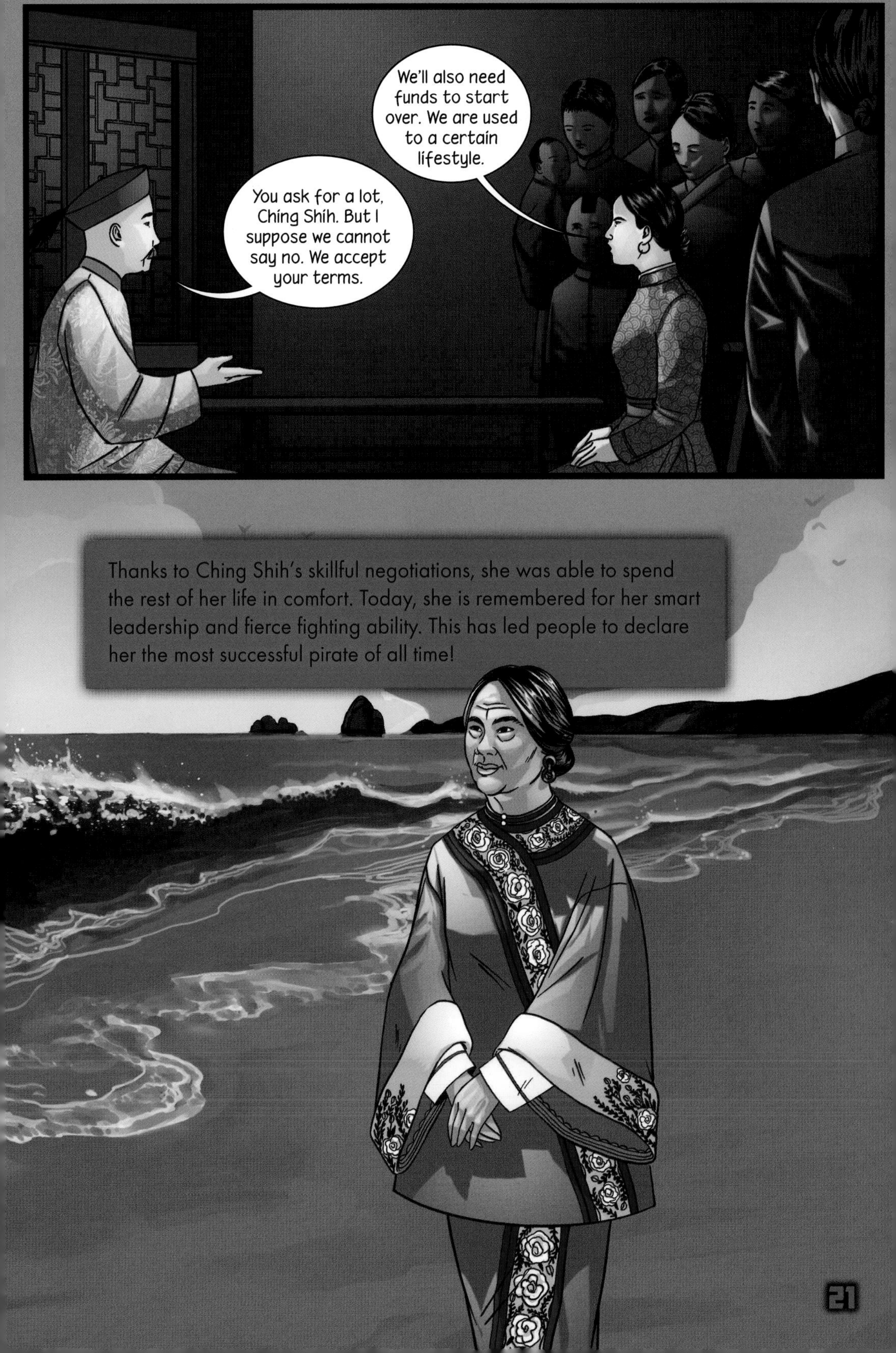

We'll also need funds to start over. We are used to a certain lifestyle.
You ask for a lot, Ching Shih. But I suppose we cannot say no. We accept your terms.
Thanks to Ching Shih's skillful negotiations, she was able to spend the rest of her life in comfort. Today, she is remembered for her smart leadership and fierce fighting ability. This has led people to declare her the most successful pirate of all time!

○ At the height of the confederation in 1809, Ching Shih was in control of more than a thousand junks. This meant 50,000 to 70,000 pirates were under her command. No other pirate ever had control of this many ships or pirates at once!

○ In many parts of the world, women were considered bad luck on pirate ships. Chinese pirates had no such belief, and women and children were occasionally aboard. However, few held the power that Ching Shih held.

○ Ching Shih and Cheung Po Tsai got married. Cheung Po Tsai later became a respected admiral in the military.

○ In Ching Shih's time, women who lost their husbands were discouraged from remarrying. They were expected to live with their husband's family.

Timeline

1807: Ching Shih takes over her late husband's position

1809: The Red Flag and Black Flag Fleets battle, with the Black Flag Fleet as the victor

1844: Ching Shih dies at age 69

1809: Ching Shih reaches the height of her power

1810: Ching Shih surrenders to the government on April 20

Ching Shih's Travels

Canton (Guangzhou)

South China Sea

Naozhou Island

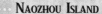

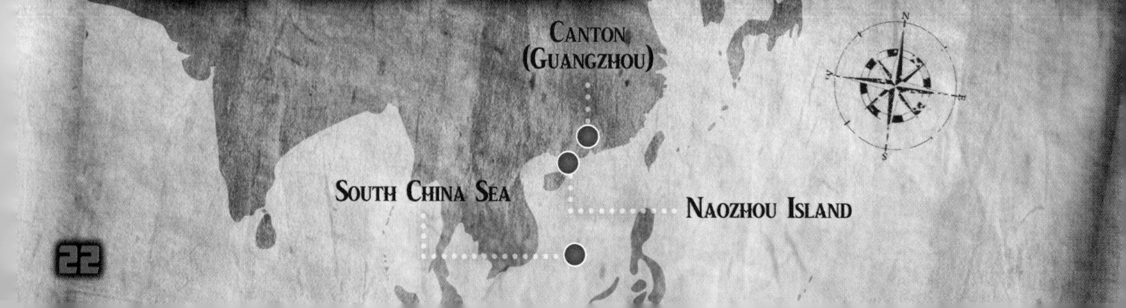

GLOSSARY

ambassadors—people sent to represent their country

blockade—a group of ships used to seal off an area, such as a harbor, to prevent people and goods from leaving or coming into the area

compromise—to come to an agreement by each side giving up something

confederation—a group of people or organizations that are joined together in the same activity or goals

cooperation—the act of working together

fleet—a group of ships under one leader

hostages—people who are taken as prisoners unless another party gives into the taker's demands

imperial—related to an empire; an empire is a country or group of territories under one ruler called an emperor.

junks—sailing ships popular in China

negotiations—discussions that are meant to bring about an agreement

pardon—an official forgiveness of all wrongdoing

protégé—a person who is trained and protected by a person of more experience

saltern—a place where salt is made

surrender—the act of giving up

terrorizing—controlling through acts that create fear

violence—acts that cause harm

23

TO LEARN MORE

AT THE LIBRARY

Chambers, Anne. *Pirate Queen of Ireland: The Adventures of Grace O'Malley*. Cork, Ire.: The Collins Press, 2014.

Leaf, Christina. *Mary Read: Pirate in Disguise*. Minneapolis, Minn.: Bellwether Media, 2021.

Steer, Dugald A. *Pirateology*. Cambridge, Mass.: Candlewick Press, 2006.

ON THE WEB

FACTSURFER

Factsurfer.com gives you a safe, fun way to find more information.

1. Go to www.factsurfer.com
2. Enter "Ching Shih" into the search box and click 🔍.
3. Select your book cover to see a list of related content.

INDEX